Unblend & Befriend

CONVERSATIONS WITH YOUR AUTHENTIC SELF

An Unbelievable Freedom® Journal

Copyright © 2022 Unbelievable Freedom
All rights reserved.
Designed and formatted by Eled Cernik.
ISBN-13: 978-1-954248-09-0

*Self has clarity that the parts do not have.
Self is in the present and parts are often stuck in the past.
Parts have their own specific agenda, but the Self's agenda
is for healing and reconciliation of the system.*

~TAMMY SOLLENBERGER, *THE ONE INSIDE*

Introduction

Greetings, Freedom Seeker.

Welcome to *Unblend & Befriend: Conversations with Your Authentic Self.*

This Unbelievable Freedom Journal was created for those who utilize the Internal Family Systems (IFS) therapeutic framework. It was designed as a self-directed tool. It is an adjunct to, not a substitute for, working with a certified IFS therapist.

You can use the pages in this journal to document the dialogue between your Authentic Self and your varied inner parts

Unbelievable Freedom thanks Tammy Sollenberger, Certified IFS Therapist for consulting on this project. Her book *The One Inside: 30 Days to Your Authentic Self* inspired the idea of using a journaling practice to let parts communicate in writing.

Setting The Stage

In your exploration of IFS, you've come to understand that we all have proactive parts that protect and reactive parts that rescue.

You've likely identified a few of your dominant or most active parts, and even given them names. This journal invites your authentic Self to invite your parts to the page.

Examples of their names might be the "Approval Seeker", "Ultra-Knowledgeable" or the "Resentment Filled One." Choose names that clearly capture their role without attaching too much negativity to them.

With the rest of this page, list out these parts and invite them to choose a handwriting they like to use. Ask if they prefer a pen or pencil and whether they like using a special color of ink.

Part #1:

Name:

Journaling Preference:

Part #2

Name:

Journaling Preference:

Part #3

Name:

Journaling Preference:

Part #4

Name:

Journaling Preference

Starting the Conversation

Part #1

Name: ....

Tell me about your job/role:

....
....
....
....
....
....

What do you like most about your job?

....
....
....
....
....
....

What do you like least?

....
....
....
....
....
....

When did you start doing your job- at what age or in what scenario?

....
....
....
....
....
....

What are you afraid would happen if you didn't do your job?

....
....
....
....
....
....

Is there a specific feeling you want to protect me from?

....
....
....
....
....
....

Part #2

Name: ....

Tell me about your job/role:

....
....
....
....
....
....

What do you like most about your job?

....
....
....
....
....
....

What do you like least?

....
....
....
....
....
....

When did you start doing your job- at what age or in what scenario?

....
....
....
....
....
....

What are you afraid would happen if you didn't do your job?

....
....
....
....
....
....

Is there a specific feeling you want to protect me from?

....
....
....
....
....
....

Part #3

Name: ....

Tell me about your job/role:

....
....
....
....
....
....

What do you like most about your job?

....
....
....
....
....
....

What do you like least?

....
....
....
....
....
....

When did you start doing your job- at what age or in what scenario?

....
....
....
....
....
....

What are you afraid would happen if you didn't do your job?

....
....
....
....
....
....

Is there a specific feeling you want to protect me from?

....
....
....
....
....
....

Part #4

Name: ....

Tell me about your job/role:

....
....
....
....
....
....

What do you like most about your job?

....
....
....
....
....
....

What do you like least?

....
....
....
....
....
....

When did you start doing your job- at what age or in what scenario?

....
....
....
....
....
....

What are you afraid would happen if you didn't do your job?

....
....
....
....
....
....

Is there a specific feeling you want to protect me from?

....
....
....
....
....
....

Continue the Conversation

Hello, ... It's me, Self.

What's going on right now? What do you need me to hear from you today?

Hello, ... It's me, Self.

What's going on right now? What do you need me to hear from you today?

Hello, ... It's me, Self.

What's going on right now? What do you need me to hear from you today?

Hello, ... It's me, Self.

What's going on right now? What do you need me to hear from you today?

Hello, ... It's me, Self.

What's going on right now? What do you need me to hear from you today?

Hello, ... It's me, Self.

What's going on right now? What do you need me to hear from you today?

Hello, ... It's me, Self.

What's going on right now? What do you need me to hear from you today?

Hello, ... It's me, Self.

What's going on right now? What do you need me to hear from you today?

Hello, ... It's me, Self.

What's going on right now? What do you need me to hear from you today?

Hello, ... It's me, Self.

What's going on right now? What do you need me to hear from you today?

Hello, ... It's me, Self.

What's going on right now? What do you need me to hear from you today?

Hello, ... It's me, Self.

What's going on right now? What do you need me to hear from you today?

Hello, ... It's me, Self.

What's going on right now? What do you need me to hear from you today?

Hello, ... It's me, Self.

What's going on right now? What do you need me to hear from you today?

....
....
....
....
....
....
....
....
....
....
....
....
....
....
....
....
....
....
....
....
....
....
....
....
....
....

Hello, ... It's me, Self.

What's going on right now? What do you need me to hear from you today?

Hello, ... It's me, Self.

What's going on right now? What do you need me to hear from you today?

Hello, ... It's me, Self.

What's going on right now? What do you need me to hear from you today?

Hello, ... It's me, Self.

What's going on right now? What do you need me to hear from you today?

Hello, ... It's me, Self.

What's going on right now? What do you need me to hear from you today?

Hello, ... It's me, Self.

What's going on right now? What do you need me to hear from you today?

Hello, ... It's me, Self.

What's going on right now? What do you need me to hear from you today?

Hello, ……………………………………………. It's me, Self.

What's going on right now? What do you need me to hear from you today?

Hello, ... It's me, Self.

What's going on right now? What do you need me to hear from you today?

Hello, ... It's me, Self.

What's going on right now? What do you need me to hear from you today?

Hello, ... It's me, Self.

What's going on right now? What do you need me to hear from you today?

Hello, ... It's me, Self.

What's going on right now? What do you need me to hear from you today?

Hello, ... It's me, Self.

What's going on right now? What do you need me to hear from you today?

Hello, ... It's me, Self.

What's going on right now? What do you need me to hear from you today?

Hello, ... It's me, Self.

What's going on right now? What do you need me to hear from you today?

Hello, ... It's me, Self.

What's going on right now? What do you need me to hear from you today?

Hello, ... It's me, Self.

What's going on right now? What do you need me to hear from you today?

Hello, ... It's me, Self.

What's going on right now? What do you need me to hear from you today?

Hello, ………………………………………… It's me, Self.

What's going on right now? What do you need me to hear from you today?

Hello, ... It's me, Self.

What's going on right now? What do you need me to hear from you today?

Hello, ... It's me, Self.

What's going on right now? What do you need me to hear from you today?

Hello, ………………………………………………. It's me, Self.

What's going on right now? What do you need me to hear from you today?

Hello, ... It's me, Self.

What's going on right now? What do you need me to hear from you today?

Hello, ... It's me, Self.

What's going on right now? What do you need me to hear from you today?

Hello, ………………………………………………. It's me, Self.

What's going on right now? What do you need me to hear from you today?

Hello, ... It's me, Self.

What's going on right now? What do you need me to hear from you today?

Hello, ... It's me, Self.

What's going on right now? What do you need me to hear from you today?

Hello, ... It's me, Self.

What's going on right now? What do you need me to hear from you today?

Hello, ... It's me, Self.

What's going on right now? What do you need me to hear from you today?

Hello, ... It's me, Self.

What's going on right now? What do you need me to hear from you today?

Hello, ... It's me, Self.

What's going on right now? What do you need me to hear from you today?

Hello, ... It's me, Self.

What's going on right now? What do you need me to hear from you today?

Hello, ... It's me, Self.

What's going on right now? What do you need me to hear from you today?

Hello, ... It's me, Self.

What's going on right now? What do you need me to hear from you today?

Hello, ... It's me, Self.

What's going on right now? What do you need me to hear from you today?

Hello, ... It's me, Self.

What's going on right now? What do you need me to hear from you today?

Hello, ... It's me, Self.

What's going on right now? What do you need me to hear from you today?

....
....
....
....
....
....
....
....
....
....
....
....
....
....
....
....
....
....
....
....
....
....
....
....

Hello, ………………………………………. It's me, Self.

What's going on right now? What do you need me to hear from you today?

Hello, ... It's me, Self.

What's going on right now? What do you need me to hear from you today?

Hello, ………………………………………….. It's me, Self.

What's going on right now? What do you need me to hear from you today?

Hello, ... It's me, Self.

What's going on right now? What do you need me to hear from you today?

Hello, ... It's me, Self.

What's going on right now? What do you need me to hear from you today?

....
....
....
....
....
....
....
....
....
....
....
....
....
....
....
....
....
....
....
....
....
....
....
....
....
....
....

Hello, ... It's me, Self.

What's going on right now? What do you need me to hear from you today?

Hello, ... It's me, Self.

What's going on right now? What do you need me to hear from you today?

Hello, ... It's me, Self.

What's going on right now? What do you need me to hear from you today?

Hello, ... It's me, Self.

What's going on right now? What do you need me to hear from you today?

Hello, ... It's me, Self.

What's going on right now? What do you need me to hear from you today?

Hello, ... It's me, Self.

What's going on right now? What do you need me to hear from you today?

Hello, ... It's me, Self.

What's going on right now? What do you need me to hear from you today?

Hello, ... It's me, Self.

What's going on right now? What do you need me to hear from you today?

Hello, ... It's me, Self.

What's going on right now? What do you need me to hear from you today?

Hello, ………………………………………………. It's me, Self.

What's going on right now? What do you need me to hear from you today?

Hello, ... It's me, Self.

What's going on right now? What do you need me to hear from you today?

Hello, ... It's me, Self.

What's going on right now? What do you need me to hear from you today?

Hello, ... It's me, Self.

What's going on right now? What do you need me to hear from you today?

Hello, ... It's me, Self.

What's going on right now? What do you need me to hear from you today?

Hello, ... It's me, Self.

What's going on right now? What do you need me to hear from you today?

Hello, ………………………………………. It's me, Self.

What's going on right now? What do you need me to hear from you today?

Hello, ………………………………………….. It's me, Self.

What's going on right now? What do you need me to hear from you today?

Hello, ... It's me, Self.

What's going on right now? What do you need me to hear from you today?

Hello, ... It's me, Self.

What's going on right now? What do you need me to hear from you today?

Hello, ... It's me, Self.

What's going on right now? What do you need me to hear from you today?

Hello, ... It's me, Self.

What's going on right now? What do you need me to hear from you today?

Hello, ... It's me, Self.

What's going on right now? What do you need me to hear from you today?

Hello, ... It's me, Self.

What's going on right now? What do you need me to hear from you today?

Hello, ... It's me, Self.

What's going on right now? What do you need me to hear from you today?

Hello, ... It's me, Self.

What's going on right now? What do you need me to hear from you today?

Hello, ... It's me, Self.

What's going on right now? What do you need me to hear from you today?

Hello, ………………………………………….. It's me, Self.

What's going on right now? What do you need me to hear from you today?

Hello, ………………………………………………. It's me, Self.

What's going on right now? What do you need me to hear from you today?

Hello, ... It's me, Self.

What's going on right now? What do you need me to hear from you today?

Hello, ... It's me, Self.

What's going on right now? What do you need me to hear from you today?

Hello, ... It's me, Self.

What's going on right now? What do you need me to hear from you today?

Hello, ... It's me, Self.

What's going on right now? What do you need me to hear from you today?

Hello, ... It's me, Self.

What's going on right now? What do you need me to hear from you today?

Hello, ... It's me, Self.

What's going on right now? What do you need me to hear from you today?

Recommended Reading & Resources

Boundaries for Your Soul: How to Turn Your Overwhelming Thoughts and Feelings into Your Greatest Allies, Alison Cook, PhD

No Bad Parts: Healing Trauma and Restoring Wholeness with the Internal Family Systems Model, Richard Schwartz, PhD

The One Inside: 30 Days to Your Authentic Self, Tammy Sollenberger, MA

IFS Institute website:
https://ifs-institute.com/

To continue your Unbelievable Freedom journey,
check out all our titles at
www.unbelievablefreedom.com

Made in the USA
Middletown, DE
08 July 2022

68835966R00064